Baby Flamingos at the Zoo

Cecelia H. Brannon

Enslow Publishing
101 W. 23rd Street
Suite 240
New York, NY 10011
USA
enslow.com

Published in 2017 by Enslow Publishing, LLC.
101 W. 23rd Street, Suite 240, New York, NY 10011

Library of Congress Cataloging-in-Publication Data

Names: Brannon, Cecelia H., author.
Title: Baby flamingos at the zoo / Cecelia H. Brannon.
Description: New York, NY : Enslow Publishing, 2017. | Series: All about baby zoo animals | Audience: Ages 3+ | Audience: Preschool. | Includes bibliographical references and index.
Identifiers: LCCN 2015044443| ISBN 9780766075658 (library bound) | ISBN 9780766075818 (pbk.) | ISBN 9780766075252 (6-pack)
Subjects: LCSH: Famingos—Infancy—Juvenile literature. | Zoo animals—Infancy—Juvenile literature.
Classification: LCC QL696.C56 B73 2017 | DDC 591.3/92073—dc23
LC record available at http://lccn.loc.gov/2015044443

Printed in Malaysia

To Our Readers: We have done our best to make sure all website addresses in this book were active and appropriate when we went to press. However, the author and the publisher have no control over and assume no liability for the material available on those websites or on any websites they may link to. Any comments or suggestions can be sent by e-mail to customerservice@enslow.com.

Photo Credits: Cover, p. 8 Stephaniellen/Shutterstock.com; pp. 1, 3 (right), 10 JOHANNES EISELE/ AFP/Getty Images; pp. 3 (left), 22 iStockphoto.com/Michael Fitzsimmons; pp. 3 (center), 16 The Asahi Shimbun/Getty Images; pp. 4–5 Jan Sochor/LatinContent editorial/Getty Images; p. 6 Matt Cardy/ Getty Images Europe/Getty Images; p. 12 FRANCIS GUILLOT/AFP/Getty Images; p. 14 HOLGER HOLLEMANN/DPA/Getty Images; p. 18 Buddha Weerasinghe/Getty Images AsiaPac/Getty Images; p. 20 iStockphoto.com/Windzepher.

Contents

Words to Know

chick

colony

down

Who lives at the zoo?

A baby flamingo lives at the zoo!

A baby flamingo is called a chick.

A flamingo chick is born with white or gray soft feathers called down. A flamingo turns pink because of the food it eats!

A flamingo chick stays in the nest for the first week of its life. Then, it starts to walk around, swim, and play.

A flamingo chick learns to stand on one leg, like its parents. It can stand like this for hours!

A flamingo chick lives with its family at the zoo. A family of flamingos is called a colony.

A flamingo chick eats a special thick milk made by its parents in their stomachs.

An adult flamingo knows its chick by its voice. Each flamingo makes a different call.

You can see a flamingo chick at the zoo!

Read More

Arnold, Carline. *Flamingo*. Great Neck, NY.: Starwalk Kids Media. 2013.

Gibbs, Maddie. *Flamingos (Safari Animals)*. New York, NY.: Powerkids Press. 2011.

Pingry, Patricia A. *Baby Flamingo*. Nashville, Tenn.: Candy Cane Press. 2004.

Websites

Science Kids: Fun Flamingo Facts for Kids
sciencekids.co.nz/sciencefacts/animals/flamingo.html

San Diego Zoo Kids: Caribbean Flamingo
kids.sandiegozoo.org/animals/birds/caribbean-flamingo

Index

Guided Reading Level: D

Guided Reading Leveling System is based on the guidelines recommended by Fountas and Pinnell.

Word Count: 141